rhapsody 2015

an anthology of guelph writing

VP

Vocamus Press
Guelph, Ontario

Presented by Friends of Vocamus Press

Published by Vocamus Press
©All rights reserved

Cover image by Randy Hobson
©All rights reserved

ISBN 13: 978-1-928171-19-5 (pbk)
ISBN 13: 978-1-928171-20-1 (ebk)

VP

Vocamus Press
130 Dublin Street, North
Guelph, Ontario, Canada
N1H 4N4

www.vocamus.net

2015

Preface

The Rhapsody Anthology is an annual collection of poetry and very short prose presented by Friends of Vocamus Press, a non-profit community organization that supports literary culture in Guelph, Ontario.

The anthology is a celebration of local writing that includes both authors who are well established in their craft and those who are published here for the first time, reflecting the writers and writing that formed the literary communities of Guelph during the year 2014 / 2015.

The cover art was provided by Randy Hobson. The cover and interior were designed by Jeremy Luke Hill.

Acknowledgements

Thanks to all the contributors for sharing their work so generously. Special thanks to Randy Hobson for allowing his art to be used for the book cover. Thanks finally to all those who contribute to the literary culture of Guelph as readers, writers, publishers, sponsors, venues, broadcasters, and in countless other ways – this collection is a celebration of all that you do.

rhapsody 2015

an anthology of guelph writing

CONTENTS

Walls

Laura Furster

Laura Furster studied English Literature at the University of Toronto, and has been writing and painting since childhood. She is fascinated by all aspects of the human experience, and explores it through poetry, prose, and paint.

Walls

A number of walls, surely less than ten,
stand between us. You live in your compartment,
and I in mine, and we share, in theory, the area
in between, the vicinity around – this town is ours,
yours and mine, but you and I move
through conflicting space, negatively charged,
the particles vibrating like trembling fingers.
We collide infrequently, rarely with purpose.
When we do, we meet like conductors.
Your energy leaps to form a current,
but the circuit remains slightly detached,
only sometimes rattling closed with a jolt, by accident.

Winter Renovations
Sheila Koop

Sheila Koop writes poetry, short stories, bits of creative non-fiction and is currently working on a novel for pre-teens. Her poem "Purple Voyage" won first prize at the Elora 2003 Writer's Festival Competition, and her short story, "The Arcana of Living Springs", was awarded Honourable Mention for the 2014 Elora Writer's Festival competition.

Winter Renovations

Foundations exposed, stripped;
rough floor, timber ceiling,
ailing concrete blocks who
strain to support everything on top.

A knock at the dust-clogged door,
two women with benign smiles
handing out invitations
to Jesus Christ's Memorial, April 13,

11a.m. – we'll be busy painting
over the phone messages from Fido,
cleaning up the calendar
buried under tools these last months.

All this change and renewal
seems to be too much for the house;
her legs buckle and her spirit
shakes every time the screw gun fires.

A freshet of sun warms the panes
and the sofa where I have escaped.
Taking time to run on about life's hard
course, as I sip fragrant tea,

rest my eyes with a butterfly massage,
dream of dragonfly love flitting
around the tip of our purple canoe –
My hands grip a wheelbarrow full of hope,

so rich with heavy loam,
if we can just get
it to the flowerbeds
who are in-waiting with us.

Chequeov
Nicholas Ruddock

Nicholas Ruddock is author of The Parabolist *(Doubleday 2010) and* How Loveta Got Her Baby *(Breakwater 2014).*

Chequeov

In 1904, there was a premonition of madness in the air. It was easy for him to make up that story about tuberculosis, his spitting of blood, his slow decline and death, with champagne, in Badenweiler, Germany. Instead, Anton Chekhov shaved off his moustache and left for Canada, to Weyburn, Saskatchewan. The note he left for his wife, Olga, upon the dresser in the hotel in which he "died", has ever since been suppressed by her family.

In Weyburn, he put away his fountain pen and resumed the practice of medicine. He took his thick accent, his glasses, his bandages, his stethoscope, and out into the prairie he went. He rode on his horse, Zorky, and took his time. At night, the prairie sky had taken a shift to the west. Polaris was over there now, otherwise it was all the same, even the owls. He actually made some money so he opened up a bank account. They mis-spelled his name; he smiled at the irony. Now he was Chequeov. It was lonely in Weyburn, but the loneliness brushed off him like chaff. One day a girl came to his door, looking for housework. She was a Russian girl named Sonja. She slept on a cot in the kitchen, he in a four-poster bed upstairs. After three years of this pleasant arrangement, Sonja began to run fevers, lose weight and cough. It was like old times, back home. Soon she was bed-ridden with advanced tuberculosis, as fate would have it, and their roles in the household became reversed. Now it was the doctor who waited on the housemaid. Eventually, all she could do was swallow broth, and her face became the colour of meadow-rue. One evening, Chequeov walked outside. A soft rain was falling, so soft that the still face of his pond, fringed by cut water-grass, was barely stippled. A shroud of mayflies swept from shore to shore, dipping and twisting in the pellucid air. Some fell, some spun like the briefest of pin-wheels, and twisted there upon the grey surface. He could hear a train in the distance, the whistle, the heavy rumble of grain, iron on iron. That night, when Chequeov's neighbours heard the unfamiliar crack of a pistol, twice, they came running to investigate. Had they been familiar with his written work – an impossibility under the circumstances, his obscurity being so profound in Weyburn as to rival the obscurity of all of us today – then those neighbours could have walked, confident in the solace of what they would find.

Prior to the introduction of street-lights, in Weyburn, Saskatchewan, the aurora borealis would often be visible, particularly in autumn; it would sweep the northern sky with a sybillant green-gold hiss, like a curtain falling all night, and it would stay like that until the blaze of the sun tipped up, fired once, fired twice, upon the eastern horizon.

Three Haikus

Burl Levine

A lifelong resident of Guelph, Ontario, Burl has been involved in creative writing since graduating from Wilfrid Laurier University. His work has appeared in periodicals such as The Sovereign, Good Times, *and* Tone *and in literary anthologies such as* On the Threshold *and* Words and Wonders. *In 1994, he received the St. James' Court Award at the Orillia International Poetry Festival.*

Meteor Maze

arrays of light rays,
like bright night sprites in a maze,
constantly amaze

Wet Duet

slashing eyelashes
trisect two teardrops into
six shards of sorrow

Farcing the Issue

don't laugh, but I think
that good humour is a farce
to be reckoned with

Beijing 13
Valerie Senyk

Valerie Senyk received her BFA in Fine Arts and an MA in Drama from the University of Saskatchewan, and taught Theatre Arts at universities in both Saskatchewan and Ontario for twenty-three years. She is an actor, director, performance poet, and visual artist. She has published a collection of poetry, I Want a Poem *(Vocamus Press, 2014).*

Beijing 13

the day like the inside of a steeping teapot
you could warm a bowl of noodles
on the window ledge

a dense pall of noise
thickens at each intersection
muffling the slap of my approaching sandals

magpies in muted blues and browns
have stopped to eat inside the park;
everything feels stopped

this pencil is shhhh

Tuning Your Mandolin
James Nowak

James Nowak was raised in Hillsburgh, Ontario and has lived in Guelph for the past few years. He is currently pursuing a degree in Medieval Studies at the University of Toronto.

Tuning Your Mandolin

Already, a gate of mist
is folding itself around you:
a rib-work to cage the storm,
a house from which to conjure.

Your eyes shut, your ear
pressed to a filament of silence,
you wait and remain still
as to render yourself
recognizable to crevices in the rock face.

Negotiating a balance,
you set pearls on scale dishes
before feeding a few to the pathway.
You remember: Hansel
and his breadcrumbs
incubating in the hedgerow.

Then, like a dove into a dark hat
you vanish
and become The Bat Queen
listening for shadows,
mist condensing,
a flower on the sleeve of Night.

If you return,
the mist around you
will settle into a small pool,
and you will drop your song
like a penny,
making ripples of your own reflection.

Photo

Jayelle Lindsay

Jayelle Lindsay has studied poetry with Joan Logghe in New Mexico and Pat Schneider in Amherst, MA. She has self-published a book of poetry, Tangible Evidence, *and teaches a writing workshop,* Writing from the Body, *that references her other interests in yoga and physiotherapy.*

Moving Skipping Rope
Harold E. Edgerton, 1952

Photo

The rope
The beat
The song of the rope
The beat of the rope
On the dust
The song of the dust
The beat of the rope
The loop of the rope
In the air behind
The loop of the air
In front of the beat
The rope above
The song of the girl
In the loop of the air
The dust of the song
The toes of the girl
The beat of the rope
In the loop of the song
In the toes of the girl
In the dust
On the ground
In the smile of the rope
In the smile of the girl
In the loop
In the beat
In the song
In the air.

Armenia's Sorrow
Bieke Stengos

Bieke Stengos was born in Belgium and came to Canada as a young woman. She has published short stories and poetry in various journals. She has published two books of poetry: Transmigrator *(The Private Press) and* Abandoned by the Muse *(Vocamus Press, 2014).*

Armenia's Sorrow

To Ani
pain lies buried
deep within the sinew
of bones and flesh

She still yearns
for the towers of strength
planted firmly
in waving grasses
until a cruel wind in April
scaled the mountains
like a mournful song
that sent the swirl of dancing skirts
to fly like the dervishes
who could not save women
bent over their dead children
young men
no longer hearing
the whisper of wind
in the almond trees

How can I turn back time, she wonders
and how can I keep abandoned churches
from bleeding into the weeping earth.

Signs Like Flowers
Darcy Hiltz

Darcy R. Hiltz grew up in Nova Scotia and moved to Guelph in 2004. He holds a BA Honours in History and Sociology from Acadia University, a MLIS from Dalhousie University, and a Certificate of Creative Writing from Conestoga College. Darcy is an Archivist / Librarian at the Guelph Public Library, an amateur genealogist, and an experienced farm hand.

Signs Like Flowers

green
yellow and red
on corner beds
front yards
intersections
wild
arrangements
fighting for space
to display their
names
Blokhuis
Chamberlain
Allt
some now droop
weak
from a sudden
bloom
short season
of electoral
flowering

Alice
Sean McCabe

A longtime Guelph resident, Sean has been a writer and producer in Canadian Media and Broadcasting since 2009. After publishing the short story collection Tales of Imaginary Rebellion *in 2011, Sean has spent time working and travelling across Canada and Europe. He is currently working on a second collection of stories.*

Alice

Time doesn't stand still. It accelerates. My father said that and I never believed him. Chalking it up to a cliché uttered in smoky VFW halls. But now, standing in front of Alice, blood pouring through the knee of my torn up jeans and holding a crinkled envelope in my hand, I finally understood what he meant. The red door. The peeling white paint. The rotting front stoop. It was all a punch in the gut.

I stood motionless at the bottom of the half-paved root infested driveway, hearing only my inconsistent breathing and the swoosh of traffic growing louder, then softer as it rolled past me on the street. I balled my fists together until my knuckles matched the envelope. Trying to stop time between my fingers – if only for a brief moment. My eyes came to a stop on the mailbox and I exhaled sharply. Scraping a toe against the ruts in the sidewalk. Not knowing if the next step would be the beginning or the ending of the best days of my life.

My mind leapt to the image of her face and then to her smile. It was an innocuous smile inside of a mundane day – just one of a thousand in all of all the others we had shared, but now, it was the only one I could remember clearly. Her face was fiery; with sunglasses perched

14

precariously on the top of her head. The sun in her eyes causing her to squint uncontrollably. She leaned against a wall sprayed with the graffiti of a failed street poet. "Live everyday like it's your last," it had said. Again she had smiled, and we chuckled at the sentiment as we stole a picture beneath it.

It was the kind of unspoken silliness that some had the ability to spout with conviction, despite it's rightful place on a motivational poster. But in a way I envied that a little. Caught up in a web of neurosis and hypothetical games of what if seemed so much more crippling than the idea of living blindly in pseudo-poetic sentiment. I squeezed the envelope again, two seconds away from dropping it or burning it to unrecognizable pieces.

The artists' tagged cliché failed to mention anything about consequences and hazards. The sickness that can be bred in your soul by making that choice. It failed to mention the regret of roads not taken, or the crippling catastrophe brought upon the mind by the idea of choosing the unknown. Like all inspirations, it existed in a vacuum. I wish I knew who was responsible for the tag now. I wanted to climb the steps to their apartment and tell them how wrong they were. I took two steps forward before stumbling and catching my balance on my injured leg.

The red door. The peeling white paint. The rotting front stoop. All reminders that I never wanted the last of anything. Only the first. To live moment to moment and never be able to truly seize any of them. Existing as nothing more than a blur in the mind, allowing unrealistic romanticism to thrive. To sleep where and when I may. Because then I would never have to stare at the fading colours of the season and face the fear of what may be left behind. For a short time we knew that place. We lived in that place.

Concerning Meditation

Andrea Perry

Andrea Perry has lived on both coasts but spent most of her growing years in Ottawa, Ontario. She graduated from the Royal Military College of Canada in 2008, after which she served five years as an Intelligence Officer in the Canadian Army. She has recently retired from the Canadian Forces and made a home in Guelph to pursue a life-long love of literature and creative writing.

Concerning Meditation

didn't mean to think about that – or that –
or this – didn't mean to go down a rabbit hole –
and when all's told – at the end of the minute –
be so far gone – downstream – off course – unhappy –
miserable – didn't mean to think about you – so
gorgeous – leaving me – in a pickle – at work –
as usual – crashing my car – getting the bill – crashing
your car – watching you confirm your speculations –
about leaving me – stranded – broke – alone –
unhappy – at work – as usual – not making enough –
to make it worth it – no time – no youth – soul slipping
away – slippery thing – silly thing – buried under my
liver – napping the day away – slippers up
on my sternum – a lazy freckle – on my small intestine –
hey there – let's see – some movement – some –
sparkle – a wave – or a tickle – put your dukes up –
and stand up – for me.
      From a distance, you see, thoughts with steel toes on,
        curbing my spirit.

Impossibility
Jeremy Luke Hill

Jeremy Luke Hill is a publisher at Vocamus Press *and the co-founder of* Friends of Vocamus Press. *He teaches literature, make jams and preserves, reads continental philosophy, uses open source software, bakes bread, watches documentary film, grows trees from seed, and writes poetry, among other things.*

Impossibility

The mystery of things peels like paint,
clings to the bottom of teacups,
makes vapour trails of the clear sky
and veined deltas of river mouths,
sifts sand, flings ash, cracks porcelain,
drives worlds with lazy, reckless speed
in star-circles, lets fingers feel
the water's tain as passing time.

Terra Mater Soon
Michelle McMillan

Michelle McMillan was born in Regina, Saskatchewan and has lived in Ontario since she was five years old. She has studied writing with Melinda Burns, Lorraine Gane, and Brian Henry, and she has written a collection of poetry and memoir.

Terra Mater Soon

A swift October wind drives early snow
Slices through my solitude
as cleanly as katana through flesh and bone
I pull a scarlet shawl over my silk kimono
Seek the comfort of its weight
Evoking your image
I study your stillness
against the gathering storm

A snowflake crosses the boundary
between our worlds
Lands silent on your open palm
Absorbs into your being as
my longing sinks into your darkness
Tears fall from the edge of my abandon, pool
and slip along the curve of your forearm –
Vanish

Precious warrior, you are a dark pearl
from an unknown sea
yet my waters have washed over you
in some distant place and time
Remember your elegant contours
Your commitment to the tide

I will rise again into the billowing sky
Drip from the blushing petals of the cosmos
Flow over your devotion
Return to Terra Mater. Soon
in the brooding twilight of winter
I will transform
Lie shimmering on a field of freshly turned earth
And when the sun lights on the land
I will soften under its touch –
Surrender

Passage

David McConnell

David McConnell has lived in Guelph for almost forty years, raising a family there. He and his wife are both now retired but are active in book and film clubs. David also enjoys hiking, cross country skiing, and cycling.

Passage

I come upon you,
white-haired and prone,
embracing your shroud of sheets.
Your mouth makes soft circles of air
so as not to disturb the world.
You have grown smaller,
almost to disappearance.

I imagine you as a child
running bare legged
through fields that wave
with your swiftness,
through flowers
glad of your fleet gaze.

And then you leap the years,
etch care in your brow.
There is water in you,
and fire, and stone,
and the strength of roots,
all written now in spots of age
seen slipping into night.

Peach Tree
Nick Dinka

Nick Dinka is the communications lead at the Wilfrid Laurier University Library, where he is helping to launch a new Culture Commons. A former journalist, he was a contributing editor at Toronto Life *magazine and wrote for* Quill & Quire, The Globe and Mail, *and many other publications. His novel,* The Silver Age *(under the pen name Nicholson Gunn) was released in 2014.*

Peach Tree

At roadside there stood a peach tree, and passing by a cyclist, young and bold, reached out to pluck ripe fruit from branch. Sweet juices streaming down his chin, he crested hilltop one-handed, flying. But fingers, slick, slipped from the brake, and he ran a stop sign coming down. When the paramedic bent to breathe him back, her eyes grew wide: a sudden tang of nectar from his lips. The peach, half-eaten, had landed roadside. Its pit, picked clean by ants, bided seasons, years, became a tree. On summer days its branches, laden thick with fruit, overhung the road, beckoning.

Clouded
Cid Brunet

Cid Brunet is currently studying creative writing. She writes poetry, short stories, and the occasional 'zine. You can find some of her recent work on Strange Horizons *and* Peculiar Mormyrid.

Clouded

She covered her bitten nails with inch long plates
of oxidized copper. Upon which she affixed
embroideries of gold floss manipulated into
morning glories flourishing up the pipes of an
unholy organ. Whose engravings were cast off
to facilitate anyone with desire
plucking
out
notes
flattened
by the trauma of change.

Meanwhile, I have come to love a blood orange bird
grounded by a smog of blindness. He fluttered up
from the cracked mud cleared of topsoil to perch
in my safety.

Together, we sought unlikely unlocked gates. While the
claustrophobic descent of the vaseline sky forced us
to risk attack from a pale pride stalking the chain-link
of our enclosure. My best intentions let bird know

I could be trusted. To share with her how
this extraordinary union made the struggle
worthwhile. But she is an airship
untethered and nodding

as the unfinished sunroof leaks heat
from the coldest room in her rented house. Now
every time it rains its like she is crying on top of me.

Homecoming Ritual
Matt Payne

Matt Payne jumps between idea-based fiction, stream-of-consciousness or humourous dadaism, and pieces intended to evoke specific emotions. In all things he likes to explore the fringes of human thought, feeling, and experience. His books include Dinosaur Mountain *(a surreal skiing novella),* The Sick Book of Lies *(a collection of very short pieces), and* Robot God / Hybrid Brain *(mind bending longer stories).*

Homecoming Ritual

I shivered as my cold body encountered the warmth of my apartment, and I closed the door against the winter. I stomped the snow from my boots and untied them with numb fingers, kicked the boots into the closet, shrugged off my jacket and threw it on the back of the chair. Tuque and wool gloves I threw on the thing as I walked by, removed my keys and wallet and put them on the other thing on my way to the hall. I was so eager for warmth that I was just leaving everything everywhere, which I vowed ten thousand times not to do because then I can't find anything.

My fingers and toes had that painful numb thaw feeling as I pulled off my socks and threw them somewhere that seemed totally appropriate. I'd pick them up later. My shirt was unbuttoned by the time I reached the thermostat and turned it up to 74 (why are these things in Fahrenheit?). I hung my shirt on the thermostat.

I took an empty ice cream bucket out of the recycling bin, then I took off my pants, rolled them up, put the denim bundle in the ice cream container, filled the container with filtered water, and put it in the freezer. Future pantsicle. Removed my underwear and shoved them inside one of my boots.

Now my stuff was everywhere in the apartment and I realized that I had perpetuated that same old absent-minded habit. I couldnt help but laugh. "I'd lose my head it it wasn't attached," I said. So I removed my head and put it in a cupboard for safe keeping. I peeled off my skin, folded it, and put it in the linen closet. With no skin I was losing lots of blood so I collected the blood in another ice cream bucket (another bad habit...gotta stop eating so much ice cream) and put the bucket safely under my bed where I would surely remember where it was.

While hot bathwater poured into the tub I took out my central nervous system which twitched as I stapled it to the back of the bathroom door. My bones I wrapped in a blanket. Muscles I placed over a heater to warm up.

Then I dropped my soul into a nice, hot bath.

Argument
Paul Hoy

Paul Hoy is a poet living in Guelph. His poetry is influenced by his rural surroundings, the natural landscape and the wilderness of northern Canada. He sees the world as his love object, and his poetry feels like his life. Paul's first collection of poetry is forthcoming from Vocamus Press.

Argument

The flowers printed on your teacup
by your lips just now,
or rather the flowers on a vine
circling.
We stir.
Fingerprints mark
time,
coil away
like our faces turned to
bees, our
sweetness stuck
to darkness.
So tiny,
or rather so far,
the flowers on
your teacup
singing
distant bells
Or, the bee humming like
a spoon.

No More Decorating the Mud Man
Donna McCaw

Donna McCaw has written five books: Sing a Song of Six Packs, *which claims to remember the 1960's;* Spiral to the Heart *and* The Spell of Crazy Love, *which are both poetry collections;* Under the Apple Boughs, *shorts stories about rural living in Ontario and Saskatchewan; and* It's Your Time, *a nonfiction title about getting ready for retirement. She organizes Wordfest in April and October at the Elora Centre for the Arts, and does storytelling at various venues.*

No More Decorating the Mud Man

Cruel game over,
Clay footed cad and coward,
The man behind the curtain uncovered,
Knees knocking.
He's abandoned the love he claimed he'd discovered.
A whole past discarded.

She, left shamed and alone again.
No looking back this time
Enough salt tears shed
Move and keep moving
Keep the cold and narrow bed.
This soap opera's dead.

I Can't Sleep

Rob O'Flanagan

*Rob OFlanagan has been a newspaper reporter, photojour-
nalist and columnist for nearly twenty years. He has pub-
lished two volumes of short-fiction (*The Stories We Tell
and The Blown Kiss Collection*) and has co-authored a
book of poetry,* Open Up the Sky *(Vocamus Press, 2015).*

I Can't Sleep

Without my glasses,
the morning sun turns the distant
water tower into a lotus blossom
about to open.

Smoke spirals from a neighbour's chimney.
The crown of a pine is heavy
with cones the colour of clay.
Thick icicles curtain the window.

I don't know my birds,
but one of unknown species
sings at the front of the house,
and others sing out back.
They too seem happy about
the morning.

These days I sleep a few hours
and then wake before the sun,
filled with expectation.
There are those I hope to
hear or see in the coming day,
friends, loves I need.

The winter has been long,
the news never good.
Dire economic forecasts.
Spying operations.
Petrol bombs.
Rights as fragile as
a frozen lotus bloom.

My hope awakens me.
I can't seem to sleep
through it.

Rereading the Palimpsest

Anna Bowen

Anna Bowen is a freelance writer and editor. She has an MA from the University of Toronto in Sociology and Equity Studies in Education and Women and Gender studies, as well as a diploma in Creative Writing at the Humber School for Writers. Her writing can be found in Alternatives Journal, Geez Magazine, This Magazine, Momentum Magazine *and* Spacing. *She is co-news editor of* This *magazine.*

Rereading the Palimpsest

So now we are rereading the palimpsest
right down to its bedrock
jammed with sheet pile
a shunt in the skull, a diversion
the absence of esker
shifted sideways and dispersed.
The fingerlink of water to paper
has always been chicken-wired, silk-stripped
milled and bound
fibers and lignin slide together with a suck
and are calendared by the sun –
author of reading who coaxes shoot and word.

A Past Life?

Heather Embree

Heather Embree is a trained metaphysical healing and intuitive practitioner based in Guelph. She is currently working on a collection of poetry entitled Gringa Haikus.

A Past Life?

I was Christopher
Columbus, I'm sure
before

I sat in a school
named after him,
sadly

Watching Black kids strapped
by nuns, my eyes sting
forever

The Joke

Eoin O'Shea

Eoin O'Shea was born in Toronto but moved to Guelph when he was four years old. He enjoys canoeing and any other activity that brings him to the forest. As a young writer he hopes his travels and writing will allow him to create a more complete bio in the future.

The Joke

"Isn't that rag a little dirty?"

"It wouldn't be a rag if it wasn't." The barkeep continued to rub the cup.

"Fair enough, two beers, clean glasses." The father and son sat down.

"If the rag was clean, the glass would be too, then how'd I keep busy?" The barkeep slid a couple sweating pints towards the men.

"Pray for more customers to dirty your glasses?" The father looked surprised at his son taking a triumphant swig.

"Kid's alright."

"He's not bad." The father patted his son on the shoulder. "Tell him the joke."

"He doesn't want to hear it." The son tried to hide his embarrassment behind a pint raised to his lips.

"Come on."

"Alright, two guys walk into a bar..."

"I've already heard it." The barkeep poured himself a beer. "Here's a joke, two guys walk out of the sunlight and into a bar with only a grinning bartender inside." The barkeep took a healthy gulp. "The guys sit down smiling too, they say their gonna have a drinking contest. Shots until one guy falls down. The barkeep keeps on grinning and starts pouring drinks. The men are drinking faster than the liquor can work. They make it to twelve shots before feeling the first. But once they start feeling it they really do, you know slurred hands and clumsy words. Sixteen and one stumbles, twenty and he falls. The bartender congratulates the man still standing. That guy pays both tabs and carries his friend home. Who won?"

"That's not a joke, that's a riddle."

"And that's not an answer, old man."

"The loser won. He got drunk for free."

"No son, the winner won. It doesn't matter the cost as long as you win."

"See, there's always a lesson."

"There is, but your father's teaching you the wrong one. They're both losers."

"Then who won?"

The barkeep finished his beer and picked up the dirty rag again. "The bartender."

In a Dream
Neal Hammond

Neal Hammond was born long ago in Montreal by the rail-way tracks. He loves song, story, sport, reading, and writing. Hard times linked him with those connected to the Civil Rights Movement. His father taught him that all humans are ignited by the One spark.

In a Dream

Last night in a dream –
Rather in a vision, within a dream.
An open casket – beside an open grave.
Otis Redding was there.
Just out of sight – to my right.
    Raising his arms he said,
"Neal, ya'll gotta let your imagination soar."
And a thousand white doves rose
Into a cobalt blue sky.

Twin

Marianne Micros

Marianne Micros was an Associate Professor at the University of Guelph, teaching literature and creative writing. She is the author of the poetry collections, Upstairs Over the Ice Cream *(Ergo Productions, 1979),* Seventeen Trees *(Guernica Editions, 2007), and* The Key of Dee.

Twin

the girl is young   pretty
she stares at me from the scratched
black and white polaroid   no
identification   no date

is this you? my daughters ask me
is this me? I ask my mother
no she says *no*
that is not you

she looks so much like me
features the same   she is thinner
hair different   eyebrows thicker
I do not remember the dress
she looks gypsy-like   the way
I wanted to look   but didn't

your grandmother gave me
the picture my mother says
she is a distant cousin or something
she is not you

I cannot sleep thinking about that girl
I invent a story   believe it is true
the family secret   I had an identical twin
taken from my mother at birth   raised by
my grandmother's cousins   this explains
everything   I am crying   I miss her so
I now understand my loneliness   my endless
search   I must find her

in the morning it seems too silly
like a romance novel   one of the mysteries
I love to read   but I take the photograph
to a cousin   ask if she knows this girl
perhaps this is Sophia my cousin says
daughter of Uncle Louie and Aunt Bessie
I get her address   Sophia   wisdom
mother goddess   female companion
of God

my brother scans the picture
onto his computer   enlarges it
it is you he says

not Sophia
but a young idealistic self
I don't remember

my daughter Joy recognizes the dress
she has seen it in a bag of old clothes
in the closet   I remember it too
one of my favourites   green
light wool
I want to find it
make it fit

I look at my twin   myself
the nose the mouth the haunting
eyes   she looks at me

the longing in her eyes
the mona lisa smile
the tilted head

a woman who longs
to meet
Sophia
to be
Sophia

I lose the address
gaze into space

dreaming
always
of distant lands

9 781928 171195